1 Let's Draw!

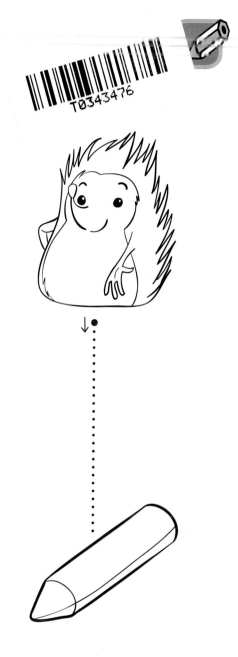

What's this? / It's a (book, teacher, table, chair, crayon, pencil).

Paint and stick leaves on the tree.

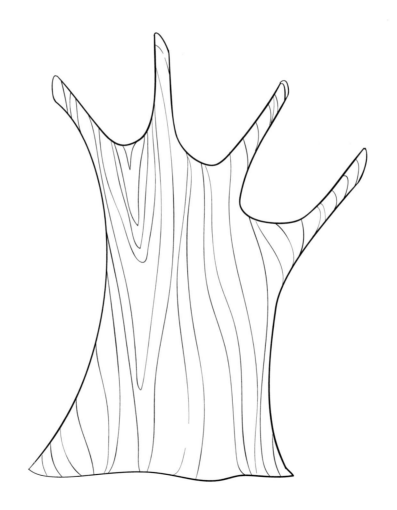

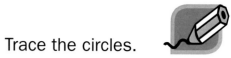

Trace the circles.

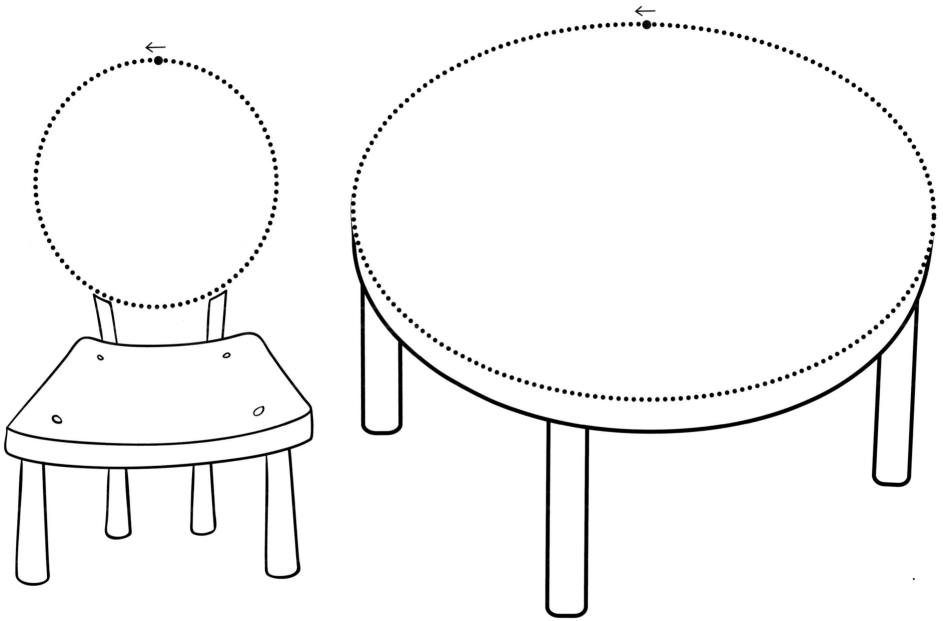

Phonics: s (Stella, snake)

2 Let's Play!

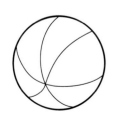   

There is one (train). / There is one (blue) (train, ball, teddy, doll, bike, car).

Find and circle the four differences.

Greenman and the Magic Forest STARTER © Cambridge University Press. **Photocopiable 6**

Trace number 1. Then colour.

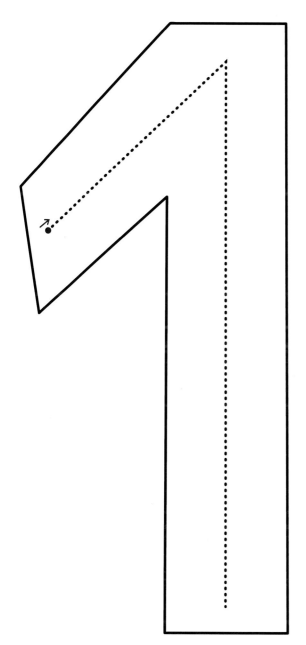

Make a book of **b** words.

Autumn Fun!

Draw, colour, cut and stick to make an autumn scene.

blue, red, autumn, happy

Greenman and the Magic Forest STARTER © Cambridge University Press. **Photocopiables 9 and 10**

Draw, colour, cut and stick to make an autumn scene.

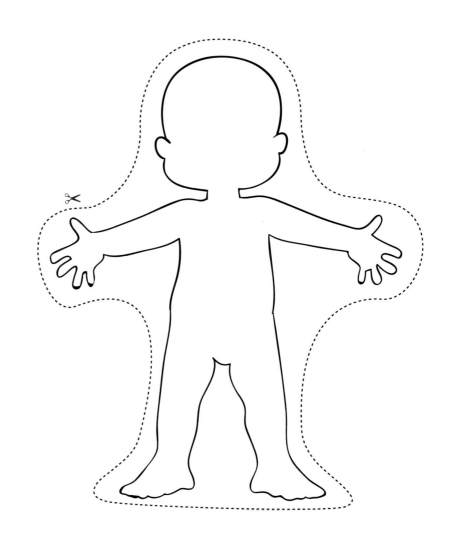

blue, red, autumn, happy

3 The Big Monster

Draw what comes next: *big* or *small*?

I can see (one) (big) (nose). / It's got (two) (small) (ear, eye, hair, face, mouth).

Greenman and the Magic Forest STARTER © Cambridge University Press. **Photocopiable 11**

Draw a monster face.

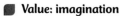

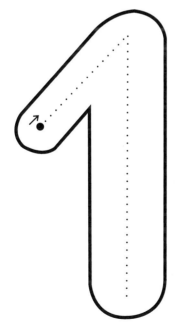

My Family

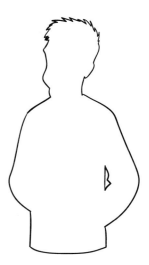

Who is it? It's (Sam's) (mummy, daddy, sister, brother, baby, friend). They look (the same).

Greenman and the Magic Forest STARTER © Cambridge University Press. **Photocopiable 15**

Find and circle the three differences.

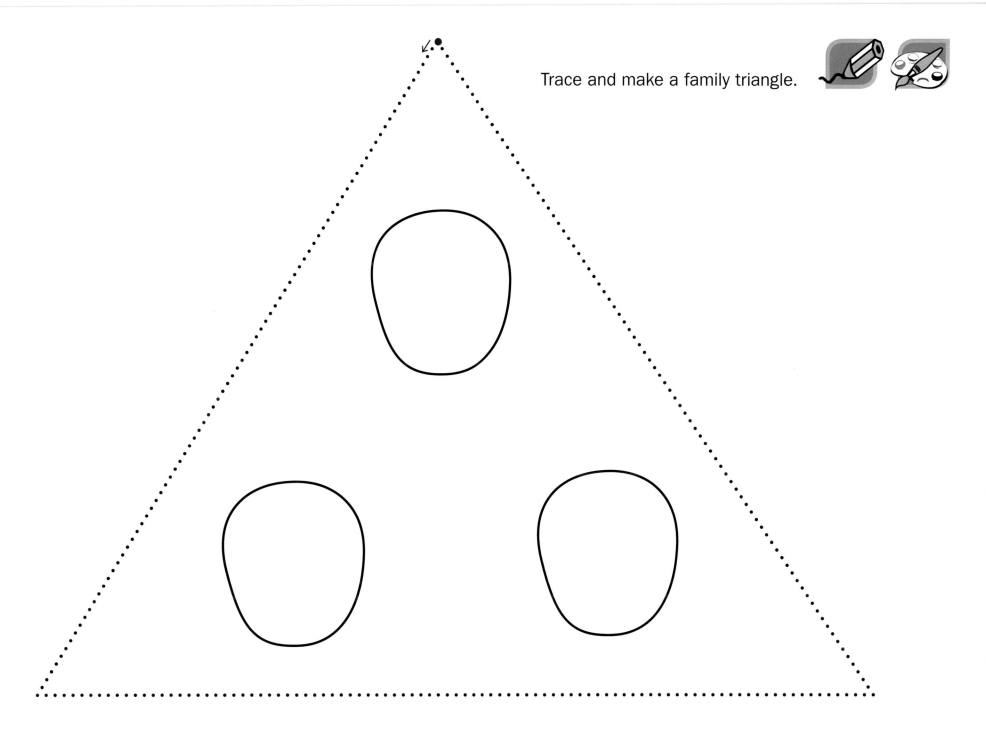

Trace and make a family triangle.

Trace the umbrella and colour the frogs.

Winter Fun!

Make a windy cloud.

Make a snowman family.

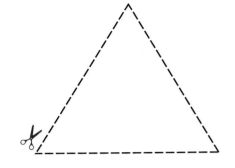
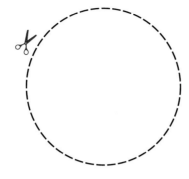

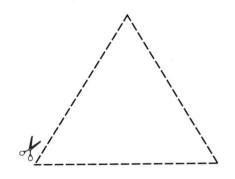
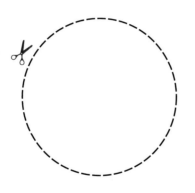
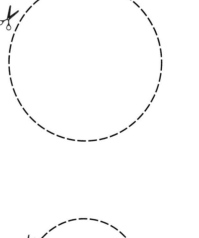
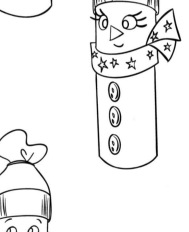

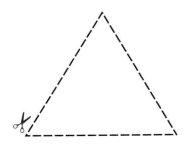

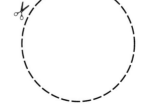

Greenman and the Magic Forest STARTER © Cambridge University Press. **Photocopiables 19 and 20**

5 Where's My Bird?

Find and circle the pets. Then colour.

Can you see your (bird, turtle, fish, hamster, cat, dog)? It's (on/under) the (table).

Help Nico find the bird.

Trace the shapes.

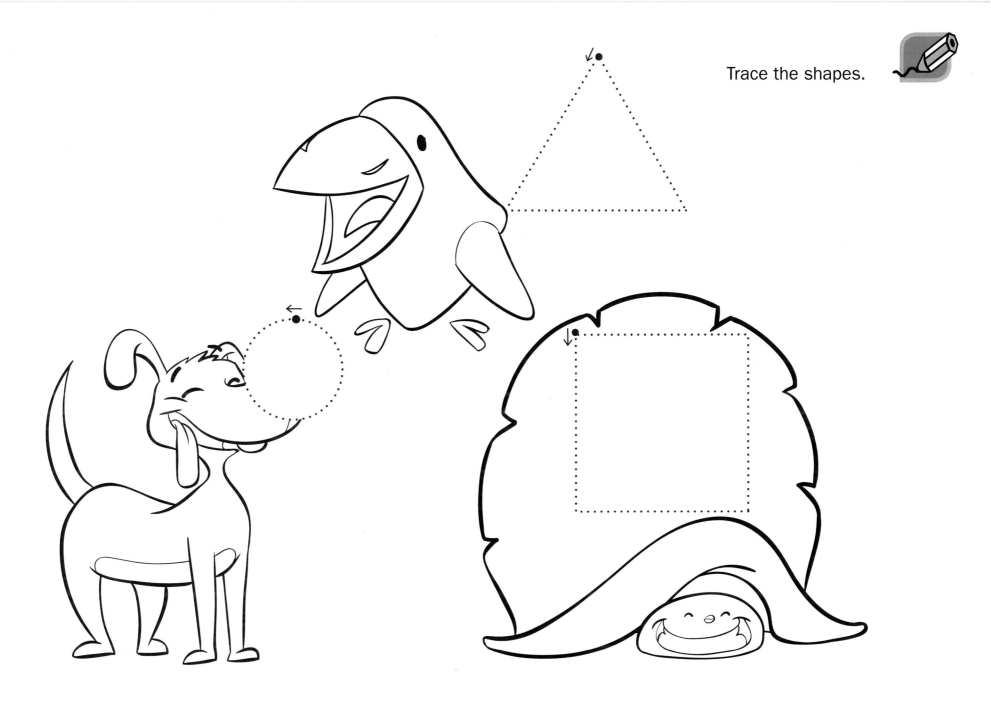

Make a kite.

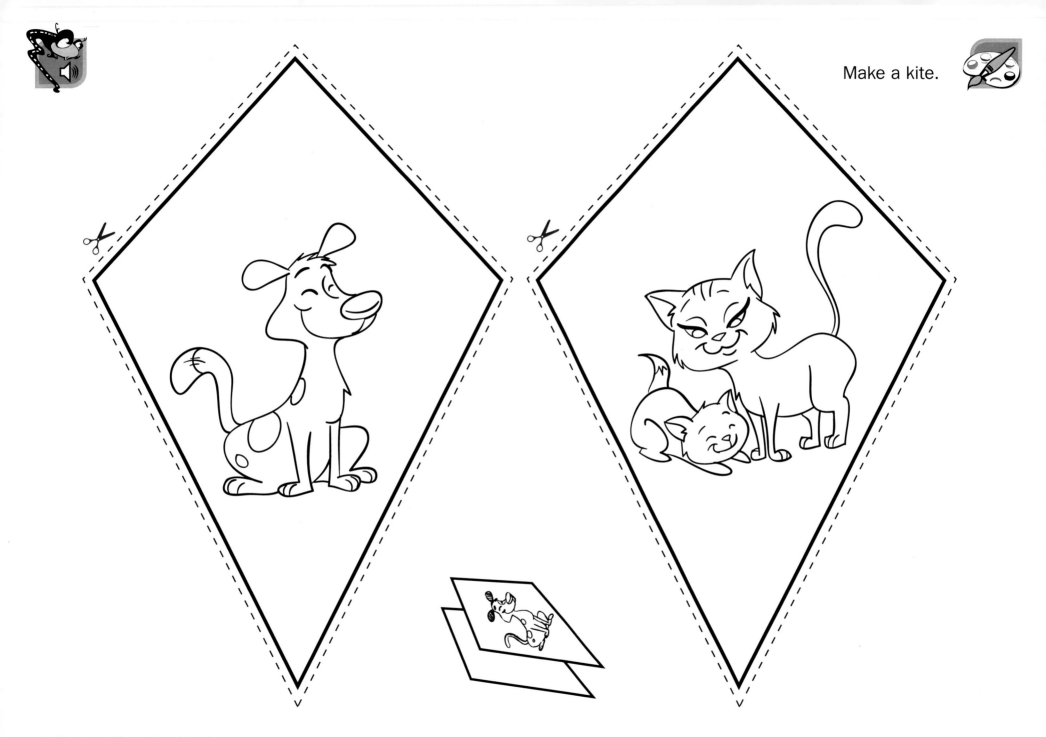

6 Let's Tidy Up!

Draw what comes next.

 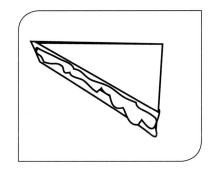  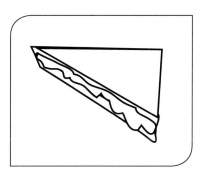

  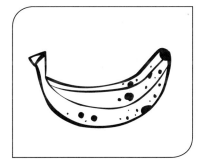 

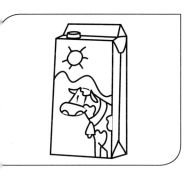   

I like (milk, sandwiches, cake, apples, bananas).

Look and match. Then colour.

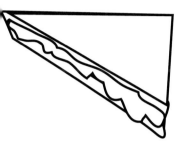

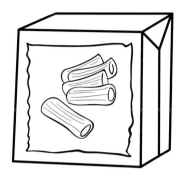

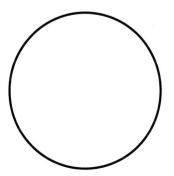
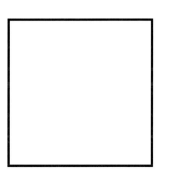
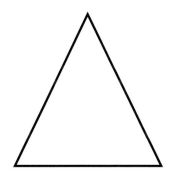
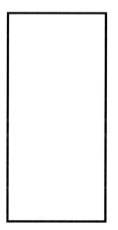

Skills: shapes

Make pasta cards.

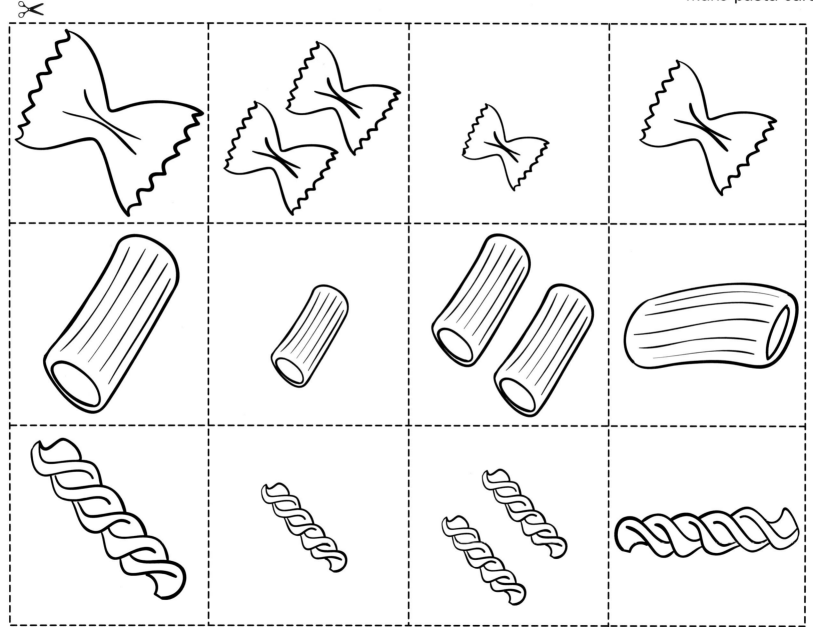

Spring Fun!

sunny, butterfly

Colour, cut and stick to make a spring scene.

Summer Fun!

Make a family chain.

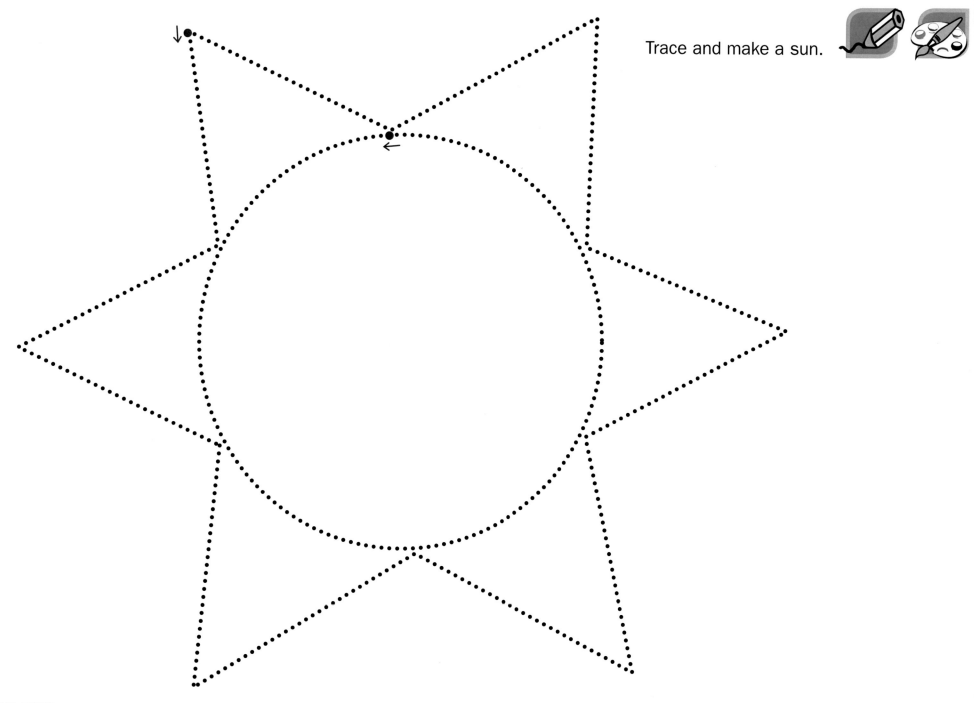

Trace and make a sun.

Congratulations!

Name _____

Halloween

Greenman and the Magic Forest STARTER © Cambridge University Press. **Photocopiable 34**

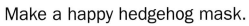

Make a happy hedgehog mask.

Christmas

Make a Christmas tree.

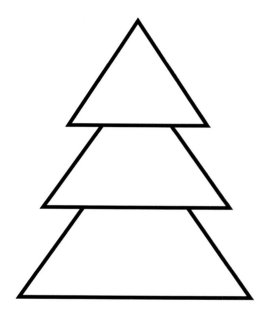

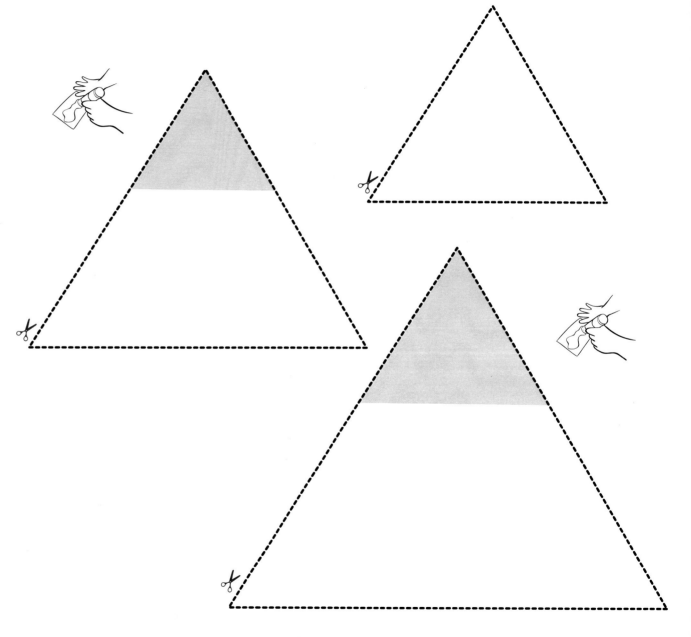

■ **Christmas, tree**

Greenman and the Magic Forest STARTER © Cambridge University Press. **Photocopiable 36**

Make a Christmas card.

r

Easter

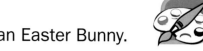

✂

Make an Easter Bunny.

Make Easter eggs.

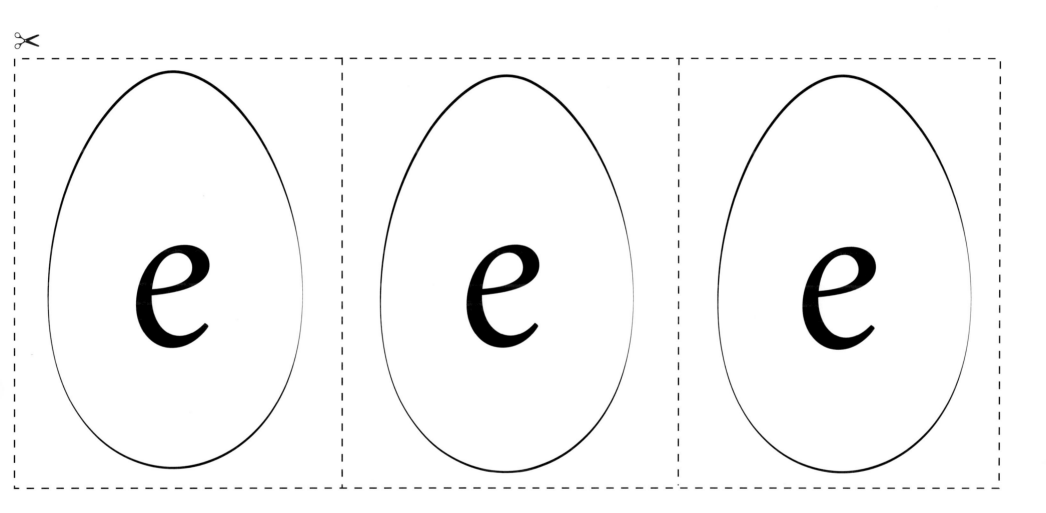

Green Day

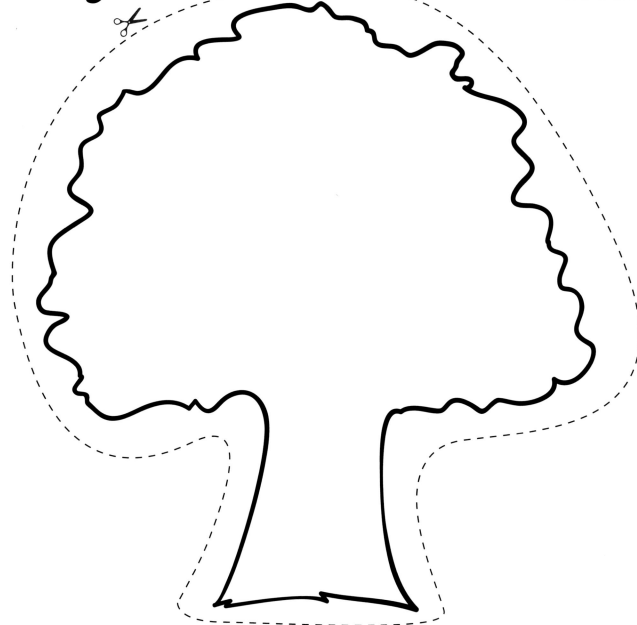

tree, forest

Make a tree train.

Goodbye!

Goodbye!

Goodbye!